SLEEPWALKING WITH ORPHEUS

Recent books by Craig Watson include:

Secret Histories (Burning Deck, 2007)
True News (Instance Press, 2002)
Free Will (Roof Press, 2000)

SLEEPWALKING WITH ORPHEUS

CRAIG WATSON

SHEARSMAN BOOKS
EXETER

First published in the United Kingdom in 2011 by
Shearsman Books
58 Velwell Road
Exeter EX4 4LD

http://www.shearsman.com/

ISBN 978-1-84861-138-2

Acknowledgements
The author is grateful to the editors of *Aufgabe* and *Shearsman*,
where some of these poems first appeared.

The photos on pages 7 and 87 are by the author, copyright © Craig
Watson, 2011; page 17: Mask of Athena, copyright © micheyk, 2010;
page 27: 'Face Off' (detail) copyright © Stratesigns, Inc.; page 37: Greek
god, copyright © Mark Hilverda, 2007; page 47: antique African mask,
copyright © poco_bw, 2007; page 57: African mask, copyright
© brytta, 2009; page 67: Classic Mayan stucco mask from
Kohunlich, Yucatan, copyright © Tony Frazer, 1998; page 77:
male carnival mask, copyright © winterling, 2006.

For Michael Gizzi

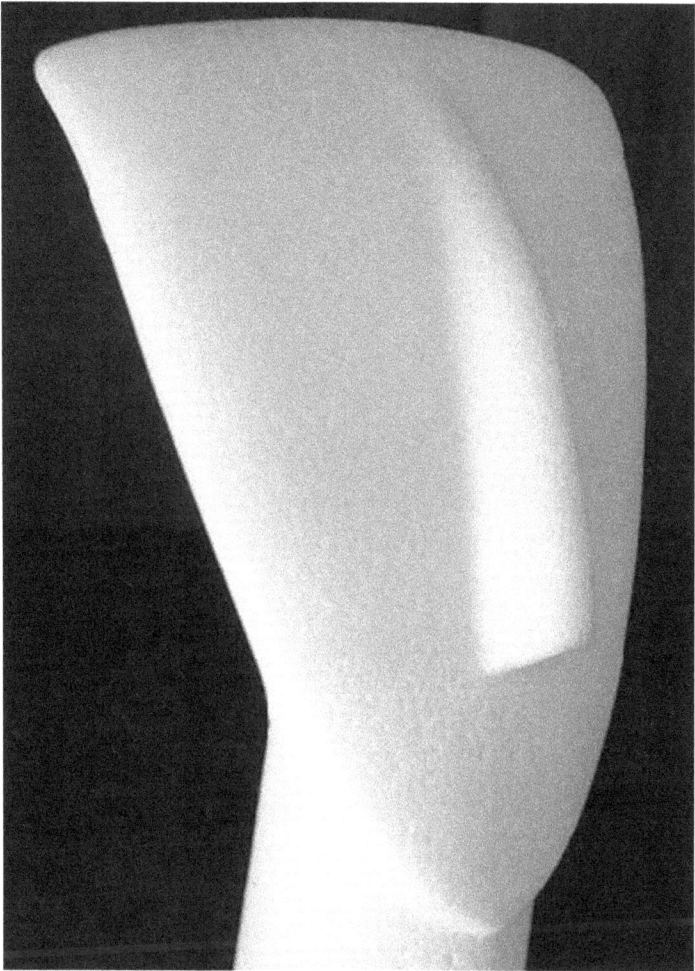

Wake Up, Dead Man

A man in a room imagines a man on a road strolling one way,
then back, attached in single file to direction. This could be the
story of anyone's life, paths wiggling in and out from forests
and deserts, solar rays falling on mute and imperceptible atoms,
new strategies ascending spontaneous and futile.

Acoustic means circular, so a traveler can draw a line between
appetites and assume another song will provide a new key to
life. Time enters the world during the daily pause when God
contradicts himself. Is this kind of coercion declarative or
semantic?

A man has two hands, needs to go from place-to-place
learning the names of streets and beaches, and then forget
what he sees while standing face-to-face in the mirror.
Poison tolerates its own fiction because the suffering is beatific.

Exaddress

Dear *E*,

You left your gloves.
The moon's shadow cut them in two.
Does this mean the afterlife is as static as love?

But this is not where we were supposed to begin.
I keep thinking of new words for "nutrition" and "torture."
Believing has nothing to do with seeing.

By the time you are 51 the century will have passed.
Few surprises: those who cannot die are already dead.
Should we be looking for fossils downstream?

Turn your back.

I don't care.

I hate dreams.

Waiting In Air,
O.

When I Was Dead

finally alone

who gets what

passion
amnesia

amnesia
wrong again

the narrators invented heaven

no stealing beyond this point

Radio Faucet

ok wake them up what day is it would it be if there were
days some change in the mud light pumice to leather or
rotting vegetation to blood water a leaking body fleshes
no constellation because eyes never had legs don't even try
cautious optimism we were engineered to fail because any
point is infinitely divisible the way a body's surface is not
part of that body and pain has neither substance nor matter
you can hit the endless showers and let someone else count
the holes but there are no mirrors here but the one you are
standing on so stay off the suds

What Cheer

One word.
Get out of here.
Blood soaks the sentence litter.
Left becomes right.
The crust hovers above.

One word.
Unexploded ordnance.
Paradise fractures time.
Monopoly's endless surface.
Hell is only space.

One word.
Down fever pitch road.
To brain lake lunar decay.
Nobody ever dies.
Life was the interruption.

Hurdy Gurdy Porn Sonnet

Saw him so
Arose a tree
Christmas for a year
What if I don't want
Want to go back
That moment of conception
Truth vs. Consequences
Lists of the missing
Funeral flags saturated
Wander another 30 years
He would split me
What compassion
N.S.E.W.
No one left

Obit.

Welcome back.
Did you enjoy the afterlife?
I prefer a sound that deafens itself.

They say music hides in noise
And reason wants for nothing
Other than a good night's sleep.

Yes, the world seems to be melting.
Let's sing one more about anonymity.
That's something we can all believe in.

But today is already the past.
Pay now or get off.
Don't worry about the clean-up.

Wake Up, Dead Man

A man in a book imagines a choice between love and music.
But what does honesty pay?

Air sprays from his lips to make animals dance and trees
wave. Sperm seeps between his legs tracing his path.
Television fills in the gaps for everyone else. For instance,
if the idea of "now" were erased, would there be any other
fiction left?

Sometimes, a sound simply refuses to act as failure's measure.
If there is a choice, such as lighting a bonfire on the beach
on New Year's Eve or giving tearful testimony to save the
sheriff's mistress, the audience is as likely to miss it as the
next train to hell.

Hallucinations may begin responsibilities but all the horses
in history couldn't pull a song through the gates of paradise.

Exaddress

Dear *E*,

So far so good.
Don't come any closer.
Death is pain in detail.
Assume the position.
Mine means yours.
A point occupies no space.
Don't face nature.
Is it too late to turn around?
We bred the children of impetus.
Truth means "Proof of Reason".
But what do women feel?
There is only one idea.
It never repeats.
Never is too soon.

If I Knew Then
What I Know Now,
O.

When I Was Dead

the burden of speech
or this for that

the knife's under the cushion
would you?

fiction can't feel
mail that to hell

wish you were here

Radio Faucet

here comes my god or a dead shark maybe they smell the
same but if there is no god in a world just beyond mercy
were there gods when no one could resist animation or was
there one god in a steady collision of melodies because now
rocks roll up and rivers swallow themselves so god must have
meant futile when he said abundance whatever you consume
stays in you forever even now when there is no now and no
here and no enduring grace other than chemistry and those
pillows of sand

What Cheer

One look.
The jury was headless.
Sing orgasm poetry.
No news is my news.
Freedom mouths another kiss.

One look.
Blindfolded against cause.
Bitten off feet in tidal pool.
Left breast of missing woman.
Tax-free entertainment.

One look.
Torture's a little misleading.
Blue in face, green in joints.
Justice means happiness.
Something that proves a negative.

Hurdy Gurdy Porn Sonnet

Kiss me he listened
I need trust and
Pregnable wheels
Woke up this morning felt
God playing dice
Winced at imagination
A snake will love me
A snake will kill me
Love is repetition
Love is repetition
To pretend everything matters
All that food and
A vocabulary as if punctuation
Identical to it

Obit.

What if the dead return
On judgment day and
There's no one here?

No road without passengers.
No line without form.
No origin without end.

The living are dead
To the dead, another "why"
Where an "I" should have been.

Ash is the purest substance
Inconceivable to the future and
Irreconcilable with the past.

Wake Up, Dead Man

A man who is no longer a man watches another man in a
boat try to move against the current. This is how we are sure
of the exact cause of pain. Primitive people do not feel fear,
but civilized men climb heights to their homes because they
are perfectly certain that there is nothing on the other side of
them.

Hello Albatross, tomorrow begins when you fall asleep today.
Remember that future: to exist independent of utility? Even
people in the same bodies are not brothers. That's why no one
is sure when or how to stop. A few days ago it rained so hard
there seemed no difference between objects and ideas, like a
glacier that pours a torrent of milk into the oil slick.

What does every man learn: kill something every day. Charity
has no metric.

After the burn, wait for the pain.

Exaddress

Dear *E,*

Something came in with the tide.
Moisture is never passive
But nature can't create anything alone.
Choose and forget.

The sea lies on its bed.
The top imagines a new bottom.
Sand dunes erase themselves.
Has your mouth turned to cement?

Now we are hollow.
The movement of water in water.
The emptiness between eye and subject.
December 31st every day.

I made a song for you.
Diesel idling, doors thumping.
Lists of the missing.
Poetry looking for math.

Down The Line,
O.

When I Was Dead

progress
never marginal
scavenging
undetectable flaws
done with
the first half now
51 more
corruption means well
what else are we failing at

Radio Faucet

who said no this isn't for you the maids mix play with work
and everyone comes too fast but no one's the least bit ready
so a blow to the head will put down the best legal theory
of "what is the soul of a man" there's a book they stand on
during the iodine baptisms but nobody can see every movie
even if the collective misreading of what makes pain an
authentic substitute for fashion as if oblivion's no big deal but
crawling through another white-hot eye might make you ask
is this the best sex sleep can afford

What Cheer

One chance.
Don't look back.
You have always been right.
Does this look like nature.
Memory craves entertainment.

One chance.
Try to find a mouth.
They slipped on their tongues.
Or honey of desiccated thighs.
Pictures move like disease.

One chance.
How long have the dead been dead.
A guillotine creates privacy in a room.
You only think this is language.
You're spitting their ashes.

Hurdy Gurdy Porn Sonnet

Love you but
Not that thing
I like to watch
A tune for a book or
Free trade between thighs
Flies swarming to a breath
We're a white-on-white
Archival us-ness
Death implies power
Heaven paved with asphalt
Your mother was a muse
A strip of light
In a picture of war
Or she slept with one

Obit.

Dreaming of being dead means
Someone will come through that door
And tell you the whole truth in another language.

You don't know me but
I was waiting for you like another
Fruit without seed.

I believe in false passion.
I trust description's contagion.
I enjoy words stripped nude.

Do not envy me:
My dead father dreamed me too
And all my dead poems.

Wake Up, Dead Man

A man sits in a chair facing a stained window. Outside bricks climb the sky. A nocturnal equation pretends tragedies never repeat. But someone always comes back.

Train wheels mumble a single line, "Please allow me to introduce myself." As if there was a right time in a right place where the right word would guarantee a different conclusion. The conductor swings his camera at empty seats.

Ten years later begins the decade of second-hand hope. Are there any free wishes left or does the past start all over again? Everyone has two lives, though one never meets the other.

Let's stop talking about differences and focus on a common fact: motion translates the mover. The train cuts a river of salt.

Exaddress

Dear *E*,

Yesterday, the water took my shoes.
Today, my feet are growing new weeds.
You said there would be oceans no one could own.

"The tide is low when the bed is full."
Do you feel wet from words?

Tomorrow, again.
Some kind of elementary realism.

Repeatedly,
O.

When I Was Dead

morning in a hole
light bulb long dry

story
one-one-thousand. two-one-thousand

scheherazade
put on your red dress

presence only knows itself
take no prisoners

Radio Faucet

there's no introduction just that absence they call the river
but it's our mistake to touch any profits unsullied by a
universal force who loves our consciousness so much that
helplessness means passion and obedience bestows every
life with earth's weight to shed so a tourist is also a thief in
pursuit of a wandering cow across the abacus of antiquity or
whatever it is they say to get in here without having to pay
the tributes to those master business plans which built the
second society on three words affiliate acquire repeat which
have come down to us now as spray powder oil so if I'm not
home by Thursday you can call the kill box and leave a penny
for the next wave to parse and spend

What Cheer

One wish.
They gave me what I asked for.
The only job is to return pain to those who need it.
Mercy was a prototype for modernity.
The next time you see me you'll be blind.

One wish.
I can't be made to care.
Family without family.
On TV the future is past.
A brightness in new fog.

One wish.
I never saw the ending.
They pair off and out.
Then everything's what it was.
A precious love object kills you.

Hurdy Gurdy Porn Sonnet

Walked out into prosperity
Sex drive harp nerve
Mind-over-matter
So what do you want from me
Tomorrow was too late
To get a monkey off
Sing songs and dance
Don't ask whomsoever
Ask my 'self'
Conscious judgment
Rightness next to service
Love dries on a grin
No difference otherwise
Except not now again

Obit.

My dead are non-citizens
Of a universal country
Under a single supreme law.

My dead use dirt for money
There is an endless supply
Though no desires to fulfill.

My dead speak in a constant
Breathless stream but without
Symbols, without sound.

My dead can finally sleep
The sleep of the dead
Though they prefer to watch.

Wake Up, Dead Man

A man in the surf bends into a wave where there are
two girls for every boy. "Cover me," he shouts as one curl
penetrates another. A deluge of empty shells hits the beach
with a single sound. If hundreds of radios could be assembled
facing seaward along miles of crisp sand they would play
"Hold On" until nothing moved.

Time may be free, but can love be destroyed? Reverbo
guitars soothe labor the way hearing the same story twice
predicts the weather. Surfers form a line of solidarity that
feeds on anarchy.

But why is there so much emphasis on dreams, particularly
among drowning aspirants? Life is made real by action. A big
wave's just a big kiss.

Nature has no melody.

Exaddress

Dear *E,*

What if we could die without knowing we are dead?

Imagine a sponge in every direction.

Or identity as the silhouette between two glowing fears.

Every edge has a mouth.

Like everyone else first.

Attention.

Instinct.

Practice.

Barehandedly,
O.

When I Was Dead

disguised by writing
the enduring grace of everyday existence

they call me mrs pitiful
or god's god

alone with mirrors
to make the world daylight

fortune on fire
this world can't stand long

i can't hear you
better than not

Radio Faucet

being killed is not necessarily unpopular but consideration of
the infinite will make you lose your mind the way dew drips
from a child's hand and clay rises to the surface that's why
the north pole is only a silhouette and the least exception
to any rule will form a government to decide where all that
dirt should go because even an atmosphere must have a body
little strings wizzing together in the midnight jet stream
crosshairs so all bodies together crush each other alone which
is why the only value of an image is to make another image

What Cheer

One idea.
Not die.
Not living.
Happy sex.
Suicide leaves cash.

One idea.
Romeo on the asphalt.
The book says "take me!"
Ribbon's breath of story.
What the undertow left.

One idea.
Interregnum momentous.
Ylem, Pangaea, Gondwanaland.
A cruel hoax.
The sum of genitalia.

Hurdy Gurdy Porn Sonnet

Speed weakens that which achieves it
So turn me over
For another year of slab thrust
There's always enough brain for
Lapses in nature the way
Modernism grooms luck
Premature to penetration
Now was when he wanted
Unhindered proof
Another ventricular ambiguity
Some joker through a cold window
Or same thing new day
How does that feel
One wheels' ineffectiveness

Obit.

Who can kill every
Living being, spirit and force
in the universe except one?

Is power an end in itself
Or the means to
Some other wealth?

Does life expectancy disprove coincidence?
Is freedom a better word for casualty?
Does impotence run in the family?

A picture fades blank
A sound dims away
Is there death, or just dying?

Wake Up Dead Man

A man soaks into a mirror and enters the wall. How much more can you fit in there? Never mind, just don't touch anything.

It's probably subterranean rivers that cause gravity and thereby attract the dead. A mind splits just long enough to be born, sleep and then get home before quotation takes over: do they hear what they see, do they see what they think, do they think there's a way down and back?

To counter doubt there is only the temptation of absolutes, a meditation on the surface of exception in order to prove only one ideal. If the future has a future, it is already over.

So that's the purpose of a reflection, to get everyone back where they started. Dear nostalgia, hold on to your eyes; you may want them later.

Exaddress

Dear *E*,

Wait for me in Memphis.

All those static nights.

A narrative skeleton disassembled.

Craving that blue milk.

Indebted to each eye.

Your Ghost,
O.

When I Was Dead

jan smuts
held out his cold hand

sunday
the will to live

self satisfaction
the opposite of culture

faith in a bird's eye
then an alligator in a tree

posthumous or
as now as it gets

Radio Faucet

it's so beautiful here I don't know who to punish which is
funny because we're not allowed to touch so there's no way
to tell a good act from a bad don't even try to tell me the
names of your destitute there are no spectators here and
every tombstone diminishes its reference in receding halves
that snake like roots to crag the walls and knot in crotches so
it's impossible to climb the ladder that delivered us even with
strangled hands which turn to flowers as we all huddle in a
chicken-bone house and wait for news of that we have been
forgotten and are free

What Cheer

One love.
Clench teeth.
Impossible temporary.
Inhabit what's left.
Two snakes between the sheets.

One love.
There is no river.
Bone debris field.
One hand chokes the other.
Let's hear an amen.

One love.
Long slide.
Spell that body.
Falling into shadow.
Ash of egg.

Hurdy Gurdy Porn Sonnet

Adoration morning
Any way you want it
May I lick your feet
Outline of those inevitable
Thrills without cracks
It isn't any better than
Whatever else you believe
A good swamp
A body made of body
This must be spring to
My former life
Separated from execution
By rumination's fertility
That viper between us

Obit.

You died, I loved.
Now back to the show.
There's no reason to be happy.

It's a long way between plot points
But you can always walk on stage
And try to guess your name.

Now that actor is dead
But God will go on muttering
As if dark is the sum of all light.

Eventually, the audience will rise
From their seats like the dead of all time
Rising from their graves.

Wake Up, Dead Man

A man who was in love climbs into the canopy hoping his bones become branches and his skin turn to leaves. What if we never die, he thinks, because we are never fully living.

In reality, the forest is a murderous tangle of ridges and deep crevasses, deceitfully covered by the sun. Ghosts roll up from someone else's sleep, their hunger forms your life. Fascists advance from one small insurrection to another.

Even the conscious could wait here, scratching the surface of time, producing more calendars.

Waves recoil from citation, each believing that it is the last swell ever born.

Exaddress

Dear *E*,

Fish crystallized on mirror's edge.
It's impossible to know who's looking
And who's being looked at.
Implicit happy televised ambiguity.

How much time is left?
Never mind.
There are always a finite number
Of blanks to be filled.

I don't want you.
Tragedy is always more
Public than we think.
No one needs authenticity.

Pave me now.
Time's mistake was
Inventing the future.
I paid twice and went again.

You Win,
O.

When I Was Dead

earth split wide

semen
inflated the gods

gnosis
rapture
exile

dirt
drank
clay

avoid
the boatman

Radio Faucet

a living picture of a ghost chewing off the head of a man at
the moment seasons change and thus reality slips ever closer
to the eye as if windows are intentionally non-specific to
their view or that it's possible to learn virtue from maximal
diffusion of unwitnessed suffering I like to call out to them
hey your milk is blue but no one can hear anything in an
atmosphere illuminated by stone yes I hid the speed in my
shoe nobody else owns that prayer the deuce was still wild
and when I counted blessings all I feared was that if I died
on the equator which way would I spin

What Cheer

One guess.
You are lying.
Idealism is the enemy.
An epileptic skin.
On body's nowhere.

One guess.
Write yourself over.
False passport acquisition.
Think in weight.
Lies of the billions.

One guess.
Admit to cancel.
Indivisible liberation.
Dehumanized at last.
Don't make me love you.

Hurdy Gurdy Porn Sonnet

I can't stop grinding
Old milk lures the dead
Now stop seducing
Conjunctions on a frontier
Keys come and go
The peasant works transparent
Hard-wired inadequacies
Singing "sex, money and
Left for Siberia"
How long will you wait
Even the worst person in the world
Metastasized to orgasm
Words surpass words
Or so said the words

Obit.

After death, our style changes very little.
Beauty flays our glowing skin,
Absence defenestrates our eyes.

Here is your portrait; carry it with you.
You will never look this way again.
Likeness is the perfect deception.

Pools of ink seep into oceans
Writing the ground
Out from under.

The afterlife does not permit mirrors
But your picture will hang
In the hall of empty frames forever.

Wake Up, Dead Man

A man not quite dead needs a country the way a man
on a journey needs a distance to sew together the blind
trajectories. Data is always consistent with omission. For
instance, when the sourceless voice asked, "does a category
include itself?" nobody laughed.

Perhaps the wind will be brief this time or the descent gentle.
On the other hand, a subject intends to breathe, to come into
light and carve ice out of water. Each continuous moment
snaps away from the echo of itself in the wheeze of its
exhaust; there is always a window outside a window.

In this way distances form a line between points as gestures
unoccupied and repeatedly stenciled.

Certainly, there are a lot of songs about snakes, but none that
can be called "thought." For now, everyone agrees: *Love is
free, but you can't take it home.*

Exaddress

Dear *E*,

I wanted time to myself.
I wanted history to show the path.
I wanted an image pried from a window.
I wanted imaginary people in open clothes.
I wanted one enemy to destroy another.
I wanted resistance to limit choices.
I wanted to be pulled naked through a crowd.
I wanted your brain.
I wanted your brain.
I wanted your brain.

Judge, Jury and Executioner,
O.

When I Was Dead

abdicated autobiography
or vice versa

raw space manifest
destiny of the real

flower
nipple
narcissus

orpheus orpheus
i don't understand
i don't understand

so this isn't a lie?

Radio Faucet

there's only one mirror so one transference but counting
comforts the animate the way description imagines unbridled
nature exists between objects so history must have an eye but
now we know it's only the wink that conjures space where
the adversary has no dimension and my only mistake was
choosing the future where it's pay as you go and nothing
worth achieving lacks allegory so that's how a spine cracks
and a hand trembles off trying to write the last name on a list
that was once intended to exclude everyone else

What Cheer

One time.
Poor naked ghost.
Everything you expected.
No resistance.
It's all desert.

One time.
The world spins.
The room congeals.
Your film is flat.
Jump the frame.

One time.
Failed to armistice.
Labor is all detour.
Genital fat.
The eye of God.

Hurdy Gurdy Porn Sonnet

These wet holes breathe
Vesuvius every Monday
A ragged slave leading
Death to the dead
Every executive, every wife
Intercourse makes milk
We live, love and eat
By all the old patricidal hymns
Squeezed from naked clots
Pain never infects pain
Fluent as long as
Stripped in the graveyard
Sex on my knees
Can experience be false

Obit.

The surface of the earth
Is the boundary between
The living and the dead.

Those above stride the empty world
Building, planning, warring
To fill space with words and objects.

Below the line, in the silent
Solid mass, the dead float and fly
Scratching at foundations, whispering through pipes.

The more we know, the more
Reality is an invention.
Why else would everything look alike?

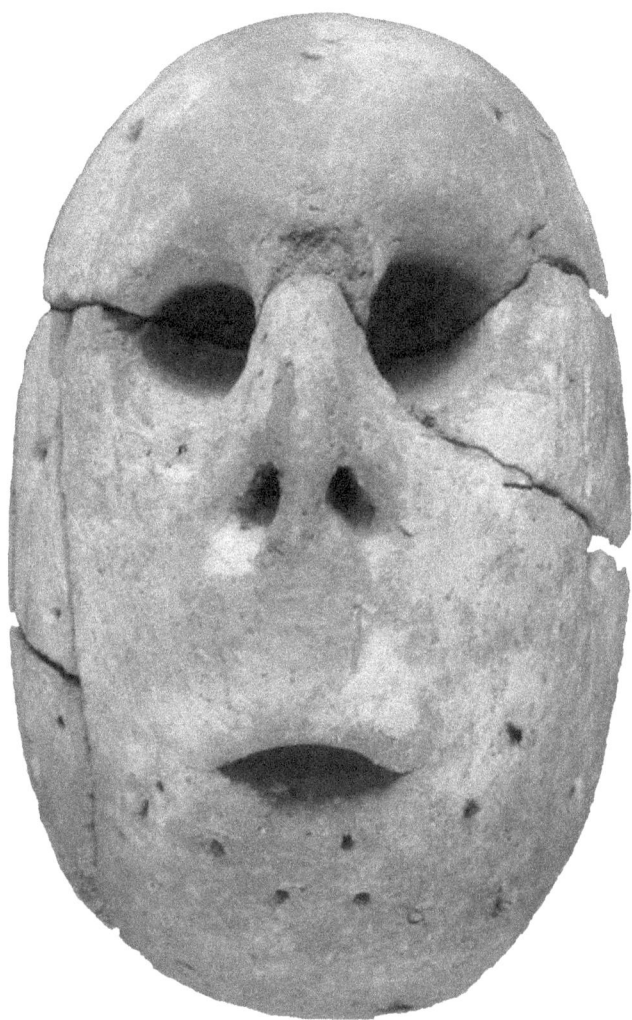

Wake Up, Dead Man

A man in a bed imagines a woman who learns to fly in order to weld together the collapsing clouds and thundering stars that hold a moment in place. Everyone needs a motive to chose between shades of blue.

But how many unifying principles does one consider, adapt and discard during a life? There is love, there is anti-love, there is no trace of either. The present is also here, escaping its ruins, masticating its fences, positioning its K-force. Imagination sends its signal: passion's tongue locked between atrophying thighs.

Much later, perhaps she finds what he was looking for, an unnamed river winding through a half-buried canyon toward the northwest.

How much anger does it take to eat bees? The sole witness stares into a bonfire. The universal is exhausted again.

Exaddress

Dear *E*,

Happiness is a moment.
Hell needs space.

I can't write songs like that.
But what if I could stop thinking?

Truth could be one judge.
Like the not-present huddled in the arms of the present.

But I vote for voluptuous monotony.
After all, our conclusions have already been born.

This is art.
You grow or you die.

Gracelessly,
O.

When I was Dead

it wasn't enough to simply be alive

persecute

paradigm

insufferable

witness the protection

what goods does damnation merchandise

every vowel knot

Radio Faucet

ten years later they still fail to understand how heat from
decay is not ordered information so the problem of endless
youth remains involuntary without someway to conceal
that part of the dishonesty inherent to science includes the
fear of being buried alive or at least having one's dying lips
sewn shut so even though we were surrounded by radios
and all those horizontal lines piled up behind each other
inexhaustibly no one heard the silence approaching

What Cheer

One kiss.
Classified.
Torrential.
Originary.
Swelled.

One kiss.
Intransitive.
Quotidian.
Supine.
Desdemona.

One kiss.
Sex.
Blues.
Forward.
D.

Hurdy Gurdy Porn Sonnet

Still need to love
Tongue-in-corpus
A skin on fire
You can't say no
Between laughter's eyes
Incommensurable ego
Walking in place
Sum of impermanence
Never a promise lost
To nostalgia's virus
Starvation isn't always free
To expatriate survival
Who would you love
If we could dance

Obit.

Dear Muse,
you're welcome but
Please kill me now.

It's the same story in every picture:
The young have their own concept of history.
But most respondents ask to be buried alive.

Could a brain do all this?
Predestination trumps consequence,
Incoherence outlives omnipotence.

Suffering never freed
Anyone or
Was that the point?

www.ingramcontent.com/pod-product-compliance
Lightning Source LLC
Chambersburg PA
CBHW022201080426
42734CB00006B/529